Petals And Hues

Varshali Budhauliya

BookLeaf Publishing
India | USA | UK

Made with ❤ on the BookLeaf Publishing Platform
www.bookleafpub.in
www.bookleafpub.com

Dedication

To the dreamers, the seekers, and the silent observers—
who find beauty in the quiet moments and speak in whispers of color.
To the ones who carry the weight of the world,
yet still manage to see its petals and hues.
This book is for you,
a collection of verses inspired by your quiet strength and boundless hearts.
May it remind you of the delicate grace that exists within every fleeting moment.
With love and gratitude.

Preface

"Petals and Hues" is an exploration of life's many shades, both soft and stark, fleeting and everlasting. It is a collection born from the quiet spaces in between moments, the pauses in conversation, and the stillness where thought and feeling bloom. Each poem within these pages seeks to capture the subtle beauty that lies in the unnoticed, the unspoken, and the often overlooked details that shape our world.

The imagery of petals and hues serves as a metaphor for life itself: delicate yet resilient, vibrant yet fleeting. Like petals falling from a flower or hues shifting with the setting sun, the verses within this book explore the transient nature of emotions, experiences, and the passage of time. But there is also a deep celebration of the fleeting beauty in these transitions, reminding us that in every impermanent moment, there is meaning and grace.

This collection is a journey—through love and loss, joy and sorrow, light and darkness. It is for anyone who has ever paused to breathe in the scent of a flower or to witness the quiet change of light at dusk. It is for those who have felt the weight of the world but still find moments of peace in the smallest of things.

May these poems offer a soft space to reflect, to be, and to see the world through a lens of color, depth, and wonder. Let them remind you that even the most fragile moments have the power to bloom, and within them, there is beauty to be found.

With each page, I invite you to pause, reflect, and immerse yourself in the petals and hues of this poetic journey.

Acknowledgements

As I reflect on the creation of *Petals and Hues*, I am filled with gratitude for many individuals whose support, love, and encouragement have made this journey possible. This book is not just the culmination of my words but also a reflection of the collective inspiration I've gathered from those around me.

First and foremost, I would like to thank my family, whose unwavering belief in me has been a constant source of strength. To my parents, thank you for nurturing my love for words and teaching me the value of expression. To my siblings, for always being my sounding board, for your endless patience, and for believing in my voice.

To my close friends—thank you for your kindness, your laughter, and for allowing me to share my most vulnerable moments with you. Your support has been a wellspring of encouragement, especially during moments when self-doubt threatened to take root.

I would also like to extend my deepest gratitude to my mentors and fellow poets, whose wisdom, insight, and passion for poetry have inspired and guided me throughout my creative process. You have shown me the power of language and the beauty in vulnerability.

To my readers, both those who have joined me on this journey from the beginning and those who have come along recently—thank you for your trust in my words. Your presence and encouragement have given me the courage to continue writing, to continue exploring the world through poetry.

Lastly, to the universe, for the countless moments of beauty and inspiration that have shaped this book—whether through the stillness of a quiet morning or the fleeting magic of a sunset—this book is a tribute to all the colors of the world, seen and unseen.

With heartfelt thanks,

Varshali

1. I owe it to you......

I owe you all the laurel,
This feeling which is surreal.....

It's your very omni-presence,
Reaffirms your quintessence......

You illuminated path of courage,
And went on for your voyage.......

You seldom needed entourage,
As you knew it's mere camouflage.......

You were a real deal,
With that indiscreet zeal...........

Still learning from your book of life,
In which daunting spirit was rife.......

You instilled valour in your life-carriage,

Fought vigorously every challenge......

How we wished your presence,
And blessings with luminescence........

Missed you at every milestone,
But knew, you are my backbone...........

Your teachings, envisioned and endearing,
Made it all easy while steering.......

You never looked back and led by example,
When life posed perils in ample.......

I owe it to you what I am today,
And try to be the best version of self each day..........

(Dedicating my first poem to my father who must be
showering his blessings from heavenly abode......)

2. Those warm hues!

The sight of warm hues,
Cues it ensues!

The color of soul,
What's that it can't cajole!

Adorning and mesmerizing,
Ravishing and enchanting!

Who ain't bedazzled ?
Enigma which is unraveled!

Teaches us to be giving,
And cherish joy of reliving!

It's indeed larger than life,
Reminisce the moments which were rife!

3. My Guru

She believed in me,when I stopped believing myself...
She came as the light at the end of the tunnel and
harnessed my true self!

She ignited the spark,
When I was struggling in the dark!

She is epitom of knowledge,
Has millions ways to encourage!

Her divinity mesmerizes,
Her persona bedazzles!

Her calmness soothes my heart,
Her beautiful simplicity sets her apart!

Almighty, help me to make her proud,
She diffused self-doubt's cloud !

Almighty, bestow all the blessings upon her,

Let happiness touch her feet & let all the success
embrace her!

The moment she came and became my Guru
Everything good & bright started to accrue

(Dedicating my poem to my Guru, who guided me
throughout!)

4. Life is a journey

Life is a journey of all experiences,
Learning all nuances,
Not clinging onto stances,
Unlearning n unseeing instances!

Keep moving forward,
Water tells us,
Leaving behind what bothers,
Embracing what nourishes!

Nature nurtures soul,
Heals n repairs heart's hole,
Constantly ask, what's your goal?
Put on new shoes n befitting sole!

Give n take chance,
Much better than repentance,
Pick up divine cues,
That's where you find the ultimate solace!

5. The Rock

The man of grit,
The man of wit!
Believes in self,
My eternal Elf!

Impossible is nothing,
Illuminates everything!
Spreads magic,
Yet so pragmatic!

Brings out the best,
Puts wits to test!
Resilience personified,
Demeanor so dignified!

You are who you are,
I am, coz' of who you are!
You always have my back,
You, my love..my Rock!

(Dedicating my this and many poems to my husband
who had been the thought and inspiration behind the
fountain of words and feelings, ever since we met!)

6. Being Mother

Somewhere between relentless retrospection,
and intense introspection,
Those countless blessings which I discover,
That's when I became mother!

Journey between "is this right?"
To embracing what's forthright,
Learnt right virtues to cultivate and foster,
That's when I became mother!

Transition of a child into a thoughtful son,
Incessant quest that had begun,
Learnt to keep it together,
That's when I became mother!

That going through learning curve,
To turning it into vibrancy and verve,
Your innocence changed my life altogether,
That's when I became mother!

Raising God's biggest miracle,
Growing into invincible Oracle,
Watching little one turning into my teacher,
That's when I became mother!

7. Be like your father .....

Dear Son,

Be kind just like your father,

And ensure not to be addicted to kindness rather.

Dear Son,

Be extremely strong like your Dad,

Yet being vulnerable sometimes isn't that bad.

Dear Son,

Be awesome like your Papa,

And learn to solve life's miseries over a Cuppa.

Dear Son,

Learn to love like your creator,

And no need to bow down n surrender.

Dear Son,

Be perfect like him,

And don't forget...imperfection makes you authentic and

genuine.

Dear Son,

Learn to let go like our common love,

Yet not letting go what's precious is virtue up n above....

8. Water

Serene and divine,
Calm and benign,
Almighty's smile,
Admire it for a while!

Transparent and translucent,
Picturesque and quaint,
The flow so agile,
Strong yet fragile .....

Why such gush,
And so much rush?
Asks little lilly,
Tiny and silly!

One shouldn't wait,
Let go of small stuff you sweat.
Says mighty water,
Gushing way too louder...

There would be obstacle,
Yet be unstoppable,
There would be mighty fall,
Yet rise above so tall...

You'll get rock bed,
To cut and shred...
You must move forward,
Be seen and heard...

Trust your might,
Do what's right...
Embrace each challenge,
And be the Change....

9. Calm

After a stormy night,
First ray of light...
That's you.

After all glitter n glamour,
I want to be at a place to be calmer..
That's you.

After wandering around in adrenaline epitome,
I want to be home...
That's you.

After excitement n adventure,
Want peaceful nature...
That's you.

After chaos, hustle n noise,
I want much needed poise...
That's you.

After numerous disagreements n struggle,
I want cozy snuggle...
That's you.

After hurt, anxiety n pain,
I want to be back to my own n known den...
That's you.

10. Everything happens for a reason!

Everything happens for a reason,
And fills the lacuna with smiles and season!

Those acts of connecting the dots,
And slowly untangling the knots!

Carefully taking each other through blind spots,
And letting into all those afterthoughts!

Mulling over what was right and what was wrong,
Releasing each feeling which was held onto lifelong!

Reminisce all that was mesmerizing and nostalgic,
Makes one certainly feel ecstatic!

Finding answers to all "Why's",
Leads to all those sad sighs....

All that quest for answers and undue somersaulting,

Rendering fuitile and way too halting...

All that convenient camouflage,
Looks nothing but tad arbitrage...

Still building each day stronger camaraderie,
And ensuring each other's solidarity!

Each day brings new revelation,
Gives new horizon to the relation!

What's all this sharing, caring and unspoken
understanding,
Wasn't it that very bonding which was outstanding!

Therefore each moment is precious,
Feeling which is surreal and pious!

One must respect and bow down to the connection,
As it's bringing self-reflection of deepest confession!

11. Perfect Serendipity

Two unknown souls,
Feel the proximity...
Feel the connection,
That's perfect Serendipity!

For no good reason,
Missing someone builds anxiety...
You want noone but The One,
That's perfect Serendipity!

You crave for togetherness,
And lose all sanity...
Causing insane struggles,
That's perfect Serendipity!

All those what,how and why's,
That endless loop of stupidity.....
Wanting all those answers at once,
That's perfect Serendipity!

Blurred line between,
Possibility and impossibility....
Not taking a No for any answers,
That's perfect Serendipity!

12. Apologies and regrets

Apologies and regrets
bring in perspective ....
They help to heal the heart,
makes it more receptive....

Opens up the window,
for meaningful conversation....
Introspection differentiates
between speculation and revelation....

Makes one more humble,
Understanding and patient...
Throws light on all what's &why's,
Mulls over on past & present...

It purifies heart,
Rekindles souls...
Lets go off control,
Acknowledges hurt and consoles...

13. Salute

My small attempt to express our gratitude,through these words!This goes to all those, for their selfless services

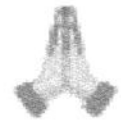

We salute your Spirit,
We salute your Grit!

It's our small Gesture,
As we all are in this Together!

It's your Sacrifice,
Which is cherishing Lives!

Here is our Applause,
For your relentless bit for the Cause!

We are so Proud,
And lauding you Aloud!

Take a Bow,
We are in your Awe!

14. The One

It felt just right,
At the very first sight.

Everything was shining and bright,
Afterall it was Almighty's might.

Hands were to be held forever,
That was the ardent wish however .

Found my THE ONE,
And life had begun!

15. Us

Sharing and caring,
Ever so endearing.

Talking and walking,
Feels so calming.

Seeing and smiling,
Each time so charming.

Feeling the depths of feeling,
Increases the longing.

Making you part of each thought,
Makes me bask in joy it brought.

16. Your Voice

Your voice,
Like a stream,
My eternal dream...
Holds my heart's realm,
Owns entire helm...

Your voice,
Windchime jingling,
Temple bell ringing,
Words start singing,
Mind starts swinging...

Your voice,
Strikes my heart's chord,
Prayers of the Lord,
My biggest reward,
My life has soared..

Your voice,
My only choice,

Which shuts all noise,
Chaos which it destroys,
Bestows upon peace and poise...

Your voice,
Makes everything right,
Shiny and bright,
Kindles soul's light,
Resonates with almighty's might

17. You and Me

You and Me,
An unknown riddle,
A sweet cuddle,

You and me,
Beautiful poem,
Says"I know him"

You and me,
Beyond rules of land,
Nothing we can't withstand

You and Me,
Purest feeling,
Hearts are healing

You are Me,
Are alter ego,
Dreams appear where we go!

18. This too shall pass

This storm will pass,
just hold on tight.

Through darkest hours,
comes morning light.

Your soul is fierce,
your heart is true,
we all believe in You.

With love around,
Huge strength and blessings surround.

(Dedicating my poem to my dear friend. She is going
through tough phase, but we all are with her.)

19. Petal

Petal,
Part of entire blooming flower,
Nature's own poetry, put together.
Delicate, fragrant and soft,
Holding tender sight aloft!

Petal,
Just like a tender memory,
Gently whispers radiant glory.
Not worried about this moment so fragile,
Hasty wind, swirling, so agile.

Petal,
Holds onto diamond dew drops,
Sun rays pass through it, time stops.
Makes best of every moment,
Turning it into grand bestowment.

Petal,
Holds innocence and purity of the universe,

Knows one day she has to dissolve n immerse.
Represents whole season's blossom,
Almighty's grace too deep to fathom.

Petal,
Knows she has to let go,
Carry on gently with wind and flow.
She played her part, it's time to depart,
Love, loose to make a fresh start,
Isn't it life's own way to train heart?!!

20. Reflection of Soul

Glass wall between two worlds,
Me and her, belong to two realms.
She knows me, I know her,
We were always in each other's prayer.

We were always together in clarity or blur,
In words' fluency or slur.
We are alter ego,
Yet resonate with different echo.

One is tender dreamer,
Full of light n heart's redeemer.
Another one is led by her aspirations,
Prefers to walk in starry constellations.

One cares about gentle rhythm of heart,
Another one is clever and smart.
One thinks way too much,
Another sprints with instincts' rush.

Both occasionally interact n have conversation,
And make astounding revelation.
We complete each other, make us whole,
We are gentle yet powerful reflection of one soul.

21. Love and Light

When heart feels overwhelmed,
Drifting through storm, utterly unhelmed,
Sending you love and light,
To guide your soul through darkest night!

When tough gets tougher,
Weather becomes rougher,
Sending you love and light,
Along with Almighty's might!

When thoughts get tangled,
Paths get further entangled,
Sending you love and light,
Have faith n hold on tight!

When chaos becomes new normal,
Peace becomes absent n surreal,
Sending you love and light,
To choose n do what's right!

When mind runs through endless maze,
And logic goes through tunnel of haze,
Sending you love and light,
Will illuminate way n sky more bright!

Close your eyes and cajole your soul,
Let dreams whisper, find your role to make you whole,
Let my love and light be your guardian angel,
Hold my hand, let world be stable to make you strongest
n capable!